Moonquake

Chapter 1: Moon Night .... page 2

Chapter 2: Quake! .... page 8

Chapter 3: The Search .... page 14

Chapter 4: Split Apart.................................... page 20

Chapter 5: The Rescue .... page 23

Written by Adam and Charlotte Guillain

RISING STARS

Chapter 1: Moon Night

"There's a special Moon Night at Planet Zoom this evening," Rav told his friends as they were playing outside. "Who wants to come?"

"Yes please!" the others replied. Rav and his friends had been to Planet Zoom many times but they'd never visited the theme park at night.

It was getting dark when they arrived at Planet Zoom. The rides looked spooky, standing still and silent in the shadows cast by the street lights.

"The show in the planetarium starts in five minutes!" boomed a voice from the speakers.

They hurried into the planetarium and found four free seats. The screen lit up with a huge image of the Moon. "Tonight we can't see the Moon," said the voiceover. "But sometimes we can see the whole Moon and sometimes we can see only part of it. Why?"

"The Moon doesn't make its own light, like the Sun does. The dust on the surface of the Moon reflects the Sun's light, and that's what makes it shine," the voiceover continued.

"I didn't know that," whispered Finn.

"The Moon spins slowly as it moves around Earth," said the voiceover.

"As the Moon travels around Earth, we can see more and more light reflected on its surface. We see a full Moon when the Sun lights up a whole side of it. Then the Moon moves on and we see less and less light, until the Moon disappears."

"We only ever see one side of the Moon," said the voiceover. "The other side is facing away from Earth."

"I wonder what the other side is like," said Tess. Stars suddenly swept across the screen and their seats tilted backwards.

We might be about to find out!

Chapter 2: Quake!

The friends found themselves spinning away into space. Just when it seemed the whirlwind would never stop, they skidded to a halt.

"What a journey!" Rav said, looking around in amazement. "Are we on the Moon?" He lifted his hands and found a space helmet on his head.

"Yes, it looks like the Moon," said Finn. "It feels like it too!" He took a huge step and bounded through the air towards them.

"I can't see Earth," said Tess, "so we must be on the side of the Moon that can't be seen from Earth."

They bounced around on the surface until a shout from Rav made them stop. "The surface is moving!" he yelled. They all stood still and then staggered as the rocks beneath their feet juddered and shook.

"What's happening?" shouted Finn.

"It feels like an earthquake!" cried Asha.

"A moonquake!"

The shaking seemed to go on forever as the friends tried not to fall over.

At last it stopped. Tess breathed out in relief. "That was scary," she whispered.

"Don't turn around," hissed Rav, "but there's something moving over there."

Everyone froze as Rav squinted into the distance.

"Aliens!" he gasped.

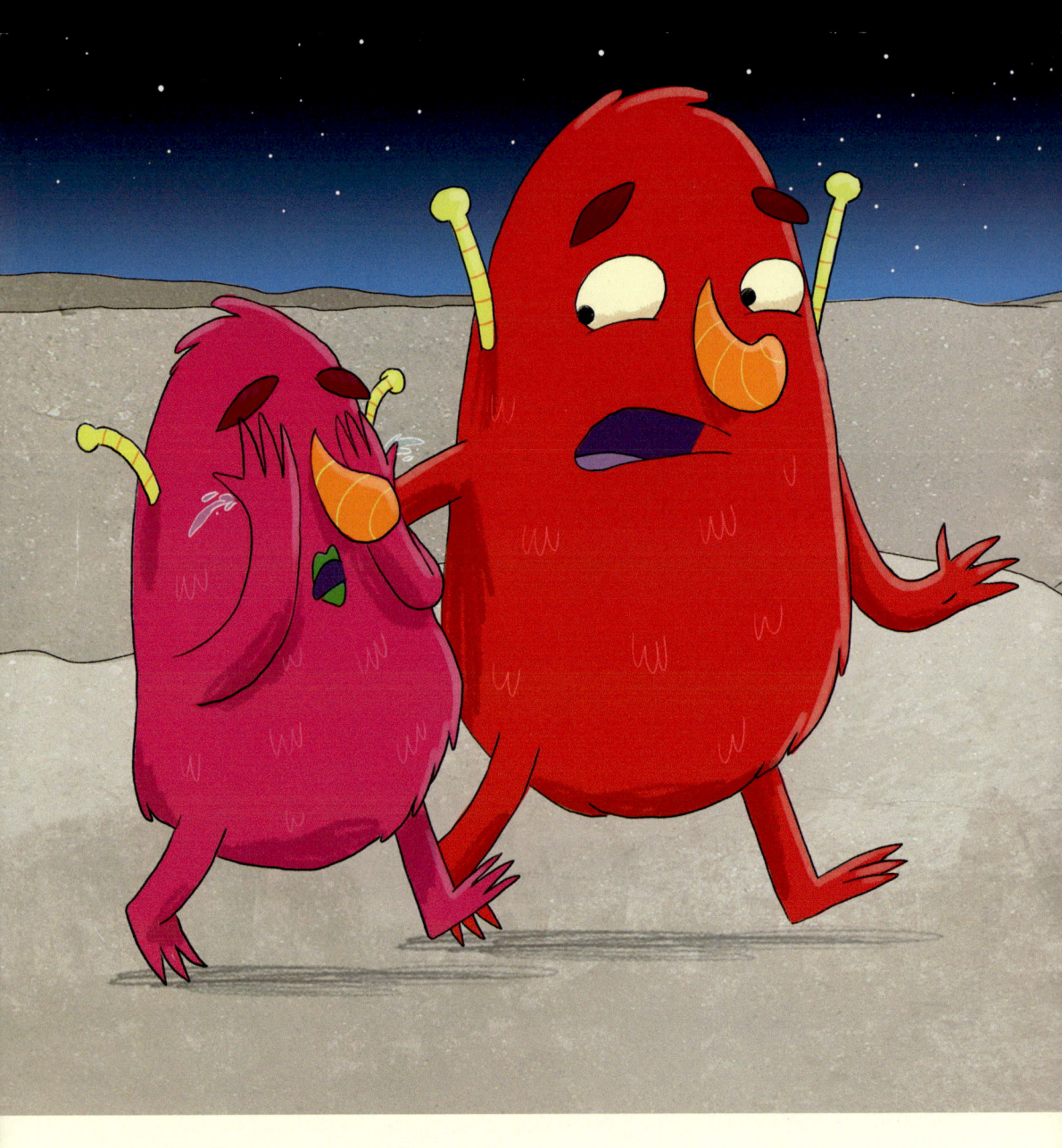

"They're huge!" said Asha. "Quick, hide behind that crater!"

The friends dashed across and peered out around the side of the crater. They watched the aliens cross the rocky landscape.

"They're looking for something," whispered Finn.

They watched nervously as the aliens moved closer. The smaller alien covered her eyes and wailed, "We'll never find her!" The larger alien hugged her as she kept crying.

"I don't think they're dangerous," whispered Asha. "Maybe they need our help."

Cautiously, the friends crept out and waved.

Chapter 3: The Search

The aliens looked up and their eyes widened. "Greetings, Earthlings!" said the larger alien. "I'm Urg and this is Norg. I wonder if you can help us?"

The friends introduced themselves. "We can try to help," said Tess with a smile. "What's the problem?"

"We were travelling across the galaxy but stopped here for a break," said Norg. "Then the moonquake happened and we lost our daughter, Snarg."

"Oh no!" said Finn.

"We'll help you look for her," Rav told them.

"There's just one problem," sighed Urg, pointing at the rising sun.

"Soon there will be too much sunlight shining on the Moon."

"What do you mean?" asked Asha.

"When too much sunlight hits the surface, it will be too hot for any of us to survive here. It gets as hot as boiling water!" said Urg.

"We have to leave before that happens," said Norg.

"Us too!" cried Finn, glancing around nervously.

"Let's start searching then," said Tess. "Where were you when the moonquake happened?"

Norg scratched her head. "Snarg was bouncing off in that direction," she said, pointing at the horizon.

"Let's go!" said Asha.

"What planet are you from?" asked Finn as they bounded across the Moon's surface with Norg and Urg.

"We're from Oggle," said Urg. "We're on our way to visit family on planet Uckjuck. That's our spaceship." He pointed up at a huge spacecraft hovering high above the Moon.

"Look!" shouted Rav, and he pointed at something moving in the distance. Urg and Norg followed Rav's gaze.

"It's Snarg!" cried Norg, and she jumped up and down and waved.

From the top of a crater, Snarg waved back. Then the ground started to shake again.

"It's another moonquake!" yelled Norg.

Chapter 4: Split Apart

Rav and Tess stumbled as the surface shuddered and jolted under their feet. "That was a p-powerful m-moonquake," stammered Rav as the ground calmed again.

"Where are the others?" asked Tess, glancing around. "What if they're hurt?"

Rav frowned. "We need to find them before it gets too hot!" he said.

Asha and Finn couldn't see Tess and Rav either. "Where are they?" said Asha.

"The Moon was shaking so much we must have got split apart," said Finn.

Nearby, Urg and Norg were getting to their feet.

"We've lost our friends too," said Asha, spinning around to look for them.

"Climb on our backs," Urg suggested. "We'll find them quicker that way!"

Finn and Asha jumped on to the aliens and they bounded across the moonscape towards the crater where Snarg had been standing.

Chapter 5: The Rescue

As they approached the crater, Norg spotted something on the other side. "Is that you, Snarg?" she called.

But it was Tess and Rav who appeared and bounced over to join them.

"We found you!" said Asha, feeling a wave of relief.

"Where's Snarg?" wailed Norg.

"Mama!" called a voice.

"She's fallen inside!" panted Urg. He looked over the side of the crater.

"Let's get her out," said Finn, following Urg. "We really need to get off the Moon soon!"

"I'm stuck!" called Snarg. She was lying at the bottom of the crater, covered in rocks.

"Don't worry, Snarg," shouted Norg.

"We'll get you out!" called Tess, then she turned to the others. "How are we going to do that?"

"Hold on to my ears," Urg said to Tess.

"What?" Tess asked, her eyes wide.

Sit on the edge of the crater and hold my ears.

Tess did as Urg said and gasped as his ears started to extend like two rubbery ropes. She held on tightly and slid down the crater towards Snarg. Snarg was crying and trembling at the bottom.

"I've come to rescue you," said Tess with a smile. "Hold on to my feet."

Moonquake

"How will you get to your spaceship?" asked Finn, looking around for a shuttle pod.

"Like this," said Urg. "Goodbye! Hold tight, Snarg!" Norg and Urg held their noses and vanished.

"We really need to get out of here too," said Rav. Just in time, stars swirled around and swept them away.

"Wait!" said Norg. "Tess, please have this to say thank you." Norg held out a shiny blue coin. "It's all I have, I'm afraid – just an Oggle pound."

Tess stared at it. "Wow, thank you! It's perfect for my holiday challenge!" Tess's class had to collect six things during the summer.

Snarg grasped hold of Tess's shoes, and Urg's ears started pulling them upwards. Tess felt stretched like an elastic band … But at last they both tumbled out of the crater.

"Thanks!" croaked Snarg. Norg lifted her up into her arms.

"We have to go!" urged Urg as the sunlight grew brighter.

What other things will the Comet Street Kids collect for their holiday challenge? Read the other books in this band to find out!

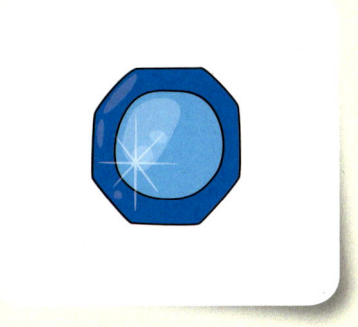

Moonquake

Brilliant Braille

Stop Shouting!

Stranded Panda

A Midsummer Night's Disaster

The Missing Cat

Talk about the story

Answer the questions:

1 What was the special event called at Planet Zoom?

2 What were the names of the two aliens the friends met on the Moon?

3 Why had the aliens' daughter got lost?

4 Why was it important that Rav, Tess and Snarg were found quickly?

5 How did Tess get into the crater?

6 What does the word 'grasped' mean? (page 27) Can you think of other words that mean the same thing?

7 Describe how you think Snarg felt when she saw her parents.

8 If you could, would you like to visit the Moon? Describe what you think it would be like.

Can you retell the story in your own words?